Week-by-Week
Poetry Frames

by Betsy Franco

New York • Toronto • London • Auckland • Sydney
Mexico City • New Delhi • Hong Kong • Buenos Aires

Teaching
Resources

To the teachers of El Carmelo Elementary School

"Sound Effects" (page 59), "Round Poem" (page 61), and "Action!" (page 63)
adapted from INSTANT POETRY FRAMES FOR PRIMARY POETS by Betsy Franco
(Scholastic, 2001). Copyright © 2001 by Betsy Franco.

Edited by Immacula A. Rhodes
Cover design by Jason Robinson
Interior design by Sydney Wright
Interior illustrations by Teresa Anderko, Maxie Chambliss, Kate Flanagan,
Rusty Fletcher, James Graham Hale, Anne Kennedy, and Sydney Wright
ISBN: 978-0-545-22305-8

4 5 6 7 8 9 10   40   18 17 16 15 14 13

Contents

Poetry Frames

Contents (continued)

Introduction

In *Week-by-Week Poetry Frames*, primary poets are encouraged to flex their creativity muscles and stretch their poetry skills. All this is done in the context of fun-filled, engaging poetry frames and starters that ensure success for everyone.

The 54 poetry frames in this book span an entire year and include four weekly poems for each month from September to August—and six extra "anytime" poems are provided for good measure! The weekly poems focus on high-interest topics, making them perfect for introducing, teaching, and reinforcing concepts and themes your students are already studying. By the end of the year, children will have a poetry collection of their own that they can reread and share with pride.

The interesting and unique formats of the frames encourage children to explore their world—from personal interests, friends, and school to animals, seasonal activities, and special days. The poems help students express their thoughts about their world, describe special occasions, imagine silly things, create new words, write observations, project their hopes and desires, share important ideas, and more.

Additionally, the poetry frames vary in complexity and in the amount of student participation, allowing you to individualize instruction. In some poems, children are asked to add only a word or short phrase, while in others, they write the entire poem.

What Are Poetry Frames?

Quick and easy reproducible "invitations" into the world of poetry. The poetry frames are simple, unfinished poems that invite students to complete them. Some have missing words; others have missing phrases. Some consist of blank lines with helpful questions and tips. All of the frames included in this collection give children the comfort of writing within a structure. They provide visual clues to help young poets brainstorm ideas and illustrate their own poetry.

Why Use Poetry Frames?

To build writing skills and meet the language arts standards. Confidence makes all the difference when a child is writing poetry. The structure of poetry frames gives students the support they need while developing a wide range of writing skills. Frames motivate young poets not only to write, but to keep writing! Using them helps students:

- write in a variety of poetry forms
- organize their ideas
- sequence events
- use pictures to describe text
- focus on specific parts of speech
- apply mechanical conventions to their writing
- write for a variety of purposes (to entertain, inform, explain, and describe)
- edit and "publish" their work
- use prewriting strategies to plan written work
- and much more!

To present a variety of poetic forms. In this collection, you'll find formal and informal poetic forms, including a quatrain, a diamante, and an acrostic poem. There are also engaging frames for writing a list poem, a letter poem, a riddle, a visual (or concrete) poem, an alliteration poem, a story poem, and poems that give directions. The different frames require varying degrees of participation from students. Some ask them to fill in words, and others invite them to write an entire poem. This variation allows you to individualize instruction because it enables everyone to participate at his or her own level.

To encourage self-expression. Using poetry frames enables students to share their opinions and imaginations about familiar aspects of their world. Children are, for example, encouraged to describe themselves, write about seasonal activities, explore weather concepts, examine animal behavior and habitats, use sensory descriptions, imagine another's point of view, and express important ideas. In addition, students are invited to let their imaginations run loose and get downright silly when they exaggerate about things they are thankful for, describe their winter holiday to an alien, write a letter from a bear's perspective, create animal valentines, and imagine what wild things might happen if 100 animals visited on the 100th day of school. The frames also encourage children to engage in word explorations, imagery, and figurative language.

To introduce basic elements of poetry. Elements of poetic language are purposely interwoven throughout this book. Examples of personification, alliteration, simile, sound words, and neologisms (made-up words) are included. Students are invited to use fun action words and interesting describing words to paint pictures with their language. They are also encouraged to play with different parts of speech—naming words (nouns), describing words (adjectives), and action words (verbs).

To build awareness of rhyme, rhythm, and repetition. Poetry frames are simply poems that need to be finished. They are structured so that they will be fun to write and to read aloud when completed. The frames often have a pattern of repeated phrase, or rhyming couplets or quatrains to begin and end poems. Some poems rhyme throughout, but in most cases, children don't have to worry about the rhyming—they can just enjoy reading their poems after completing them.

To integrate social studies, science, and math into your language arts curriculum. Poetry can so easily embrace the rest of the curriculum. In this collection, poems such as "All the Things I'm Thankful For," "Dr. Martin Luther King, Jr.," "The Fourth of July," and "My 'Me' Poem," highlight important social studies concepts. You can use "Falling Colors," "I'm a Migrating Duck," "My Teeth," and "Baby Animals" to help reinforce science skills. Additionally, "100 Guests on the 100th Day" and "At the Pond" touch on math and can be used as a springboard to explore numbers and quantity.

Using the Frames in Your Classroom

Each poem can be written individually, with partners, or as a class collaboration. Here's how you might use the frames with children:

1. Introduce the frame of your choice with the group before children begin writing. Review the directions together and write an example as a class.

2. Provide students with a copy of the reproducible frame and have them use pencil and crayons or markers to fill it in.

3. Circulate around the room to check that each child is engaged, helping to brainstorm when needed.

After poems are completed, celebrate students' efforts by inviting them to:

- share their poem with a partner or a small group
- read their poem to the class or to an older buddy
- copy their poem onto a blank sheet of paper and illustrate it as part of a display
- make their poems into a class collaborative book for the classroom library
- display their poems on bulletin boards
- take home and share their poems with families
- write their poems on blank strips, display them in a pocket chart, and chant them with the class
- act out their poems
- create their very own anthologies by binding all their poems together
- hold a poetry reading in which each child reads his or her poem to the whole class

Connections to the Language Arts Standards

This book is designed to support you in meeting the following language arts standards outlined by Mid-continent Research for Education and Learning (McREL), an organization that collects and synthesizes national and state standards.

Uses the general skills and strategies of the writing process including:

- Uses writing and other methods (e.g., using letters or phonetically spelled words, telling, dictating, making lists) to describe familiar persons, places, objects, or experiences
- Writes in a variety of forms or genres
- Writes for different purposes (to entertain, inform, learn, communicate ideas)

Uses the stylistic and rhetorical aspects of writing including:

- Uses descriptive words to convey, clarify, and enhance ideas
- Uses a variety of sentence structures in writing

Uses grammatical and mechanical conventions in written compositions including:

- Uses conventions of print (upper- and lowercase letters, spaces between words, writes from left-to-right and top-to-bottom)
- Uses complete sentences
- Uses nouns, verbs, adjectives, and adverbs
- Uses conventions of spelling (spells high-frequency, commonly misspelled words from appropriate grade-level list; spells phonetically regular words; uses letter-sound relationships; spells basic short vowel, long vowel, *r*-controlled, and consonant blend patterns)
- Uses conventions of capitalization and punctuation

Uses the general skills and strategies of the reading process including:

- Uses mental images based on pictures and print to aid in comprehension of text
- Uses basic elements of phonetic analysis (common letter/sound relationships, beginning and ending consonants, vowel sounds, blends, word patterns) to decode unknown words
- Uses basic elements of structural analysis (syllables, compound words, spelling patterns) to decode unknown words
- Understands level-appropriate sight words and vocabulary
- Uses self-correction strategies (searches for cues, identifies miscues, rereads, asks for help)
- Reads aloud familiar stories, poems, and passages with fluency and expression
- Understands the ways in which language is used in literary texts (personification, alliteration, onomatopoeia, simile, imagery, rhythm)

Source: Kendall, J. S., & Marzano, R. J. (2004). *Content knowledge: A compendium of standards and benchmarks for K–12 education*. Aurora, CO: Mid-continent Research for Education and Learning. Online database: http://www.mcrel.org/standards-benchmarks

Common Core State Standards

The activities in this book also correlate with the English Language Arts standards recommended by the Common Core State Standards Initiative, a state-led effort to establish a single set of clear educational standards whose aim is to provide students with a high-quality education. At the time this book went to press, these standards were still being finalized. To learn more, go to www.corestandards.org.

Week-by-Week Poetry Frames

It's time for a new school year!
Look around the classroom to see what else is new.
Are there new objects, people, or things to do?
Write a poem about your new school year.

Example: *New books to read.*

A New School Year

New _____ .

New _____ .

New _____ .

New _____ .

New _____ .

New _____ .

Old _____ , too.

It's a brand new year with so many things to do!

by _____

Writing only one word on each
line gives a poem some punch!
Write a poem about apples.
Use one word on each line.

Things to think about apples:
colors   tastes   sizes
shapes   ripeness

Apple Picking Time

_____

_____

_____

_____

Apples to cook and drink and eat.

Picking apples from trees is especially neat.

_____

_____

_____

_____

In all kinds of colors and shapes and sizes.

Some even have wiggly _inside_ surprises!

by _____

Write a conversation between paper and a pencil.

Pencil Talks to Paper

Paper: My job is to _____

_____.

Pencil: My job is to _____

_____.

Paper: I'm as white as _____

_____.

Pencil: I'm as yellow as _____

_____.

Paper: It tickles when you _____

_____.

Pencil: I try not to _____

_____.

Pencil: Both of us are made from _____.

Paper: Yeah, kids, recycle me. Please!

by _____

Hispanic Heritage Month starts in September.
Have fun with the Spanish words in this poem!

Speaking Spanish

Cómo está? How are you?

Speaking Spanish is _____ to do.

Uno, dos, tres means _____,

_____, _____.

Three _____

_____

in the tree.

niños

There's *abuela*. It's almost time to eat.

She is _____

for the family treat.

abuela

tacos

A taco is a mix of different foods,

_____ and _____

to name a few.

Let's learn Spanish.

Me and you!

by _____

Follow the pattern of the poem to fill in the blanks.

Knowing and Learning

I know how to _____.

I want to learn how to _____.

I know how to _____.

I want to learn how to _____.

I know how to _____.

I want to learn how to _____.

I know how to _____.

I want to learn how to _____.

The wheels in my brain turn and turn.

There are so many things that I can learn!

by _____

Comparing is a good way to describe something in a poem.
   Example: *Leaves as purple as a hummingbird's head.*

Falling Colors

Leaves as red as _____
are twirling down.

Leaves as orange as _____
are whirling down.

Leaves as yellow as _____
are swirling down.

Then all the colors
turn crunchy _____.

by _____

Write about what chipmunks do.

Use these questions about
chipmunks to help you:
Where do they hide their nuts?
Why do they hide them?
What games do they play?
What noises do they make?
Where do they sleep?
What do they dream about?

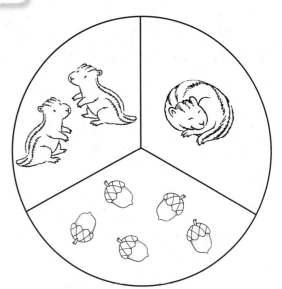

The Chipmunks' Fall Day

The chipmunks are busy throughout the day.

They must hide nuts and sleep and play.

One-third of their day, they

_____.

One-third of their day, they

_____.

One-third of their day, they

_____.

Being a chipmunk does not look very hard,

but they sure are busy in my back yard.

by _____

Week-by-Week Poetry Frames © 2011 by Betsy Franco, Scholastic Teaching Resources

A *diamante* is a poem with five lines. Write a diamante about a pumpkin. Follow the directions in the box.

Line 1: Write *pumpkin*.
Line 2: Write two things you need to grow a pumpkin.
Line 3: Write three things you would carve into a pumpkin.
Line 4: Write two words telling how the pumpkin looks with a candle inside.
Line 5: Use another word to tell about your pumpkin.

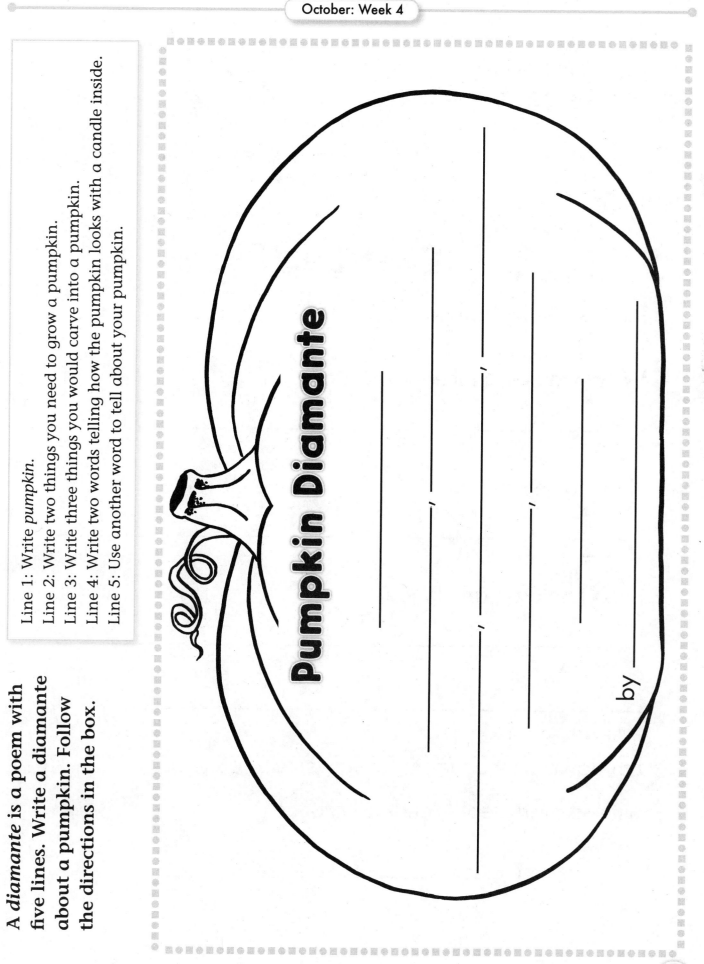

Pumpkin Diamante

by _____

Pretend it is fall.
You are the last leaf on the tree.
What is it like to be the only one?

Last Leaf

I'm the last leaf on my tree.

Way, way down there on the ground,

I see _____.

Here comes the wind.

I _____.

I can't hold on any longer.

I _____.

"_____," I shout.

I'm down on the warm, leaf-covered ground

with so many leaf friends all around!

by _____

Tell a story with your poem.

Use these questions to help you get started:
Why did the tiny bird come to the birdfeeder?
What did he want?
What trouble did he have?
How did he solve his problem?

The Tiny Bird

The tiny bird _____
_____ .

The tiny bird _____
_____ .

The tiny bird _____
_____ .

The tiny bird _____
_____ .

by _____

Exaggerate means to stretch the truth.
Use your imagination to write your poem.
Go ahead and exaggerate!

Example: *If I gathered all the things I'm thankful for
and put them in a cloud,
it would rain baseball cards and ponies.*

All the Things I'm Thankful For

If I gathered all the things I was thankful for

and grew them in a garden,

_____

_____ .

If I blew them up into the sky,

_____

_____ .

If I poured them into the ocean,

_____

_____ .

I have so much to be thankful for.

by _____

 Week-by-Week Poetry Frames © 2011 by Betsy Franco, Scholastic Teaching Resources

Poets draw pictures with words. This is called imagery.
Pretend you are a migrating bird. You are flying from a cold place
to a warm place. Use imagery in your poem.

Example: *The pond is dotted with us ducks,*
flapping our emerald and brown wings.

I'm a Migrating Duck

My friends all gather at the creek.

We sound like _____.

We _____

to get energy for the journey.

Up we fly. We take turns leading.

We look like _____.

The wind whooshes by.

I hear _____

all around me.

After many days, we are in a warmer place.

In spring, we'll gather again and return home.

by _____

You don't have to make complete sense in a poem.

You can make interesting descriptions and comparisons that way.

Example: *The bare branches are arms dancing under a winter moon.*

The hillside is a bear carrying the winter snow on her shoulders.

Winter Pictures

The bare branches are _____

_____ .

The cold is _____

_____ .

The snow is _____

_____ .

The icicles are _____

_____ .

My cold nose is _____

_____ .

I'd better go in before I turn into _____

_____ .

by _____

Sometimes a picture can inspire a poem. Draw a picture of yourself in winter clothes and color it. Use the picture to help you write the poem. Tell exactly what you are wearing.

Example: *I put on my striped red and blue scarf.*

Dressed for Winter

Before I go out on a winter day,

I put on _____

so I am warm while I play.

_____ is another

thing I wear, so I can be as snug

as a _____ bear.

And while I am building a big snowman, I keep my

_____

dry for as long as I can.

But when I'm done,

my clothes and me are as

_____ and

_____

as they can be!

by _____

In winter, it's fun to look closely at the snow!

Write about what you might see in the snow on the ground.

Example: *My boots leave fancy prints in the snow.*

Prints on Fresh Snow

The snowplow leaves

_____.

My boots leave

_____.

A dog comes bounding by, and it leaves

_____.

When I drag a bare stick behind me, it leaves

_____.

When we lie on our backs and flap our arms, we leave

_____.

So many pictures in the snow!

by _____

Poetry can be seeing something in a new way.
Imagine your family is celebrating a winter holiday.
Suddenly, a space alien appears in your home!
Describe your holiday celebration to the creature.
Begin each sentence on a new line.

Things to think about:
decorations
foods or treats
what people are wearing
traditions and routines

My Holiday Time

_____

_____

_____

_____

_____

_____

_____

_____

by _____

In poems, you can look ahead to the future.
A new year started on January 1.
What do you hope will happen this year?

A Whole New Year

A whole new year is beginning.

I hope to _____ and

_____ and play.

This year I hope to _____

on the day of my birthday.

This year, if I can get to _____,

then I will be really glad.

This year will be the _____ year

that I have ever had.

Happy New Year!

by _____

Before you write about winter, make two lists.
List the hard things and the fun things about winter.

Example: *Even though it's hard to walk through snow,*
it's great fun to build a giant snowman.

Hard things:	Fun things:

Winter Is . . .

Even though _____ ,

it's great fun to _____ .

Even though _____ ,

it's great fun to _____ .

Even though _____ ,

it's great fun to _____ .

Even though winter can be hard in some ways,

winter can be so much fun on beautiful, snowy days!

by _____

Dr. Martin Luther King, Jr. wanted everyone to get along and help each other. He wanted everyone to be treated the same.

Dr. Martin Luther King, Jr.

Dr. King would be happy to see kids

_____ on the playground.

Dr. King would be happy to see kids

_____ at our school.

Dr. King would be happy to see kids

_____ in our town.

Dr. King would be happy to see people in the world

_____ .

by _____

Pretend you are a bear that just woke up from hibernating. Write a letter to a friend. What will you write about?

Use these questions to help you:
Where were you sleeping?
What did you dream about?
How do you feel after your long sleep?
What are you going to do now?

A Letter From Bear

Dear Friend,

I _____

_____.

I dreamed _____

_____.

I feel _____

_____.

I can't wait to _____

_____.

Your friend,
Bear

by _____

A *quatrain* is a four-line verse in a poem.

The second line rhymes with the last line.

Write a poem about teeth for Dental Hygiene Month.

In each quatrain, make the very last word rhyme with the word in **bold** print.

My Teeth

When I eat _____ and _____,

my _____ help me **chew**.

So to help out my teeth,

here is what I **do**:

After _____,

I _____ and I **brush**.

I take plenty of time.

I try not to _____.

Then whenever I smile

and all my _____ **show**,

my white healthy teeth _____

and _____.

by _____

What kinds of valentines would animals write to each other?

Use your imagination and some fun rhymes!

Example: Panther to Panther

I love your claws.
I love your fur.
You are so sweet,
you make me purr.

Fun Rhyming Words

For bat:	For snail:	For fish:
ring	shell	chin
sing	swell	fin
thing	tell	spin
wing	well	win

Animal Valentines

Bat to Bat

I love _____.

I love _____.

_____

_____.

Snail to Snail

I love _____.

I love _____.

_____

_____.

Fish to Fish

I love _____.

I love _____.

_____

_____.

by _____

Use strong verbs to bring your poem to life.
Use the verbs in the box to help you get started.
Use some of your own verbs, too.

bounce	jiggle	shimmy
dive	prance	soar
flutter	shake	wiggle

Chinese New Year

Our New Year's dragons _____ and dance.

Their tails _____

as our dragons _____ .

They _____ way up,

and they _____ way down.

As we _____

our dragons all around.

Happy New Year!

by _____

Imagine 100 animals come to visit your school.
What wild things might happen?
Be as silly as you want.

100 Guests on the 100th Day

If we had 100 animal guests

on the 100th Day of School,

it could get pretty wild.

It could be pretty cool.

We would all _____

if we had 100 bees.

We would _____

with 100 chimpanzees.

The teacher says _____

if we had 100 squirrels.

She says that it is wild enough with 100 boys and girls!

by _____

It is fun to create new words!
Make up words for jobs that
the wind does.

Example: *hair-whiffler*

Think about what the wind does to:

branches	leaves	an umbrella
hair	a flag	a flying bird
hats	clothes	loose paper

The Wind

The wind has many jobs to do,

and I can think of quite a few.

It's a

_____ – _____ ,

_____ – _____ ,

_____ – _____ ,

_____ – _____ ,

_____ – _____ ,

_____ – _____ ,

and a _____ – _____ .

The wind has many jobs to do.

It's silly and wild and playful, too!

by _____

In an *acrostic* poem, the first letter of each line is used to spell out a special word.

Write an acrostic poem about spring.

This is an acrostic poem for *March*:
Melting snow clumps
Are fewer now.
Raindrops pelt the roof,
Chanting,
"Here comes spring!"

Spring

S _____

P _____

R _____

I _____

N _____

G _____

by _____

Think of three very different things you are lucky to have or to do.
Use examples that are very different from each other to add variety.
For ideas, think about your home, your school, and your friends.

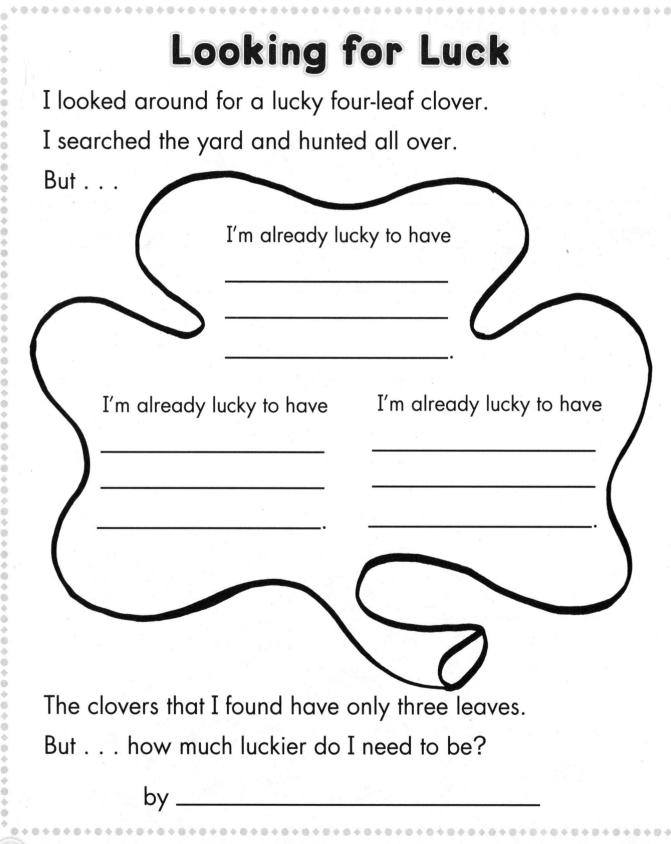

Looking for Luck

I looked around for a lucky four-leaf clover.

I searched the yard and hunted all over.

But . . .

I'm already lucky to have

_____

_____

_____.

I'm already lucky to have

_____

_____

_____.

I'm already lucky to have

_____

_____

_____.

The clovers that I found have only three leaves.

But . . . how much luckier do I need to be?

by _____

Imagine you are the spider in this poem.
You are proud of your web.
It is strong, even in wind and rain.
Use the questions in the box to help you fill in the blanks.

Example: *My spider web is like fancy lace.*

Things to think about:
Where do you like to spin your web?
What do you use your web for?
What makes it beautiful?
What shapes does it have in it?
What happens to your web in the wind?
What happens to it in the rain?

My Spider Web

My spider web is a work of art.

You know, we spiders are pretty smart.

My spider web is _____.

My spider web is _____.

My spider web catches _____.

My spider web is _____.

If my web gets ripped apart,

I get to work and make more art.

by _____

Use facts to write a poem about allergies.

Here's a fact:

Some people are allergic to new grass, tree or flower pollen, and dust in the air.

Allergies might cause people to:

sneeze	*sniffle*
get puffy eyes	*feel itchy*
wheeze	*get headaches*

Example: *When some kids stroll by springtime flowers,*
they sneeze so hard, the birds all flap their wings and fly.

Achoo! Allergies!

Sniffle, snuffle, wheeze, sneeze.

Achoo! Allergies!

When some kids walk on new-cut grass,

they _____ .

When some kids breathe the pollen from flowers,

they _____ .

When some kids play by springtime trees,

they _____ .

Sniffle, snuffle, wheeze, sneeze.

Achoo! Allergies!

by _____

What do you think the rain means to different animals?

Write a poem to share your thoughts.

April Showers

Whenever it rains, some animals play.

But other animals hide away.

The dog _____

_____.

The cat _____

_____.

The ducks _____

_____.

The mice _____

_____.

And me? I feel free

to run and jump and splash with glee!

by _____

Poetry can be used to spread the word about important ideas.
Write a poem about taking care of our planet Earth.

This Is Our Earth

These are my oceans filled with

_____.

These are my mountains filled with

_____.

This is my sky filled with

_____.

These are my jungles filled with

_____.

This is my Earth.

I take care of her.

So I recycle _____.

I re-use _____.

I use less _____ and _____.

This is my Earth and it's your Earth, too.

Let's do whatever we can do.

by _____

 Week-by-Week Poetry Frames © 2011 by Betsy Franco, Scholastic Teaching Resources

This poem has a chorus that repeats.
Before each chorus, write a verse about
a baby animal.

You can write about the animals in the box,
or think of some of your own.

Baby Animals

bunny	gosling	owlet
calf	kid (goat)	piglet
colt	kitten	puppy
duckling	lamb	tadpole

Example: *Baby ducklings paddle and eat,*
all in a row, down the creek.

Baby Animals

_____

_____.

Baby animals are everywhere.
They romp, they swim, they fly in the air.

_____

_____.

Baby animals are everywhere.
They romp, they swim, they fly in the air.

_____

_____.

Baby animals are everywhere.
They romp, they swim, they fly in the air.

by _____

It's fun to write a poem as a list of directions.
Write a poem that gives directions for a May Day parade.

Directions for a May Day Parade

1. Start with a band with _____

   and _____.

2. Next, bring on the _____

   that are _____

   and _____.

3. Have kids riding _____

   decorated with _____.

4. Line up pooches on leashes wearing _____

   _____.

5. Serve food such as _____

   _____ and give prizes away.

6. Yell "Yippee yay!" for the May Day Parade.

   by _____

Write a poem about things you can do for Mother's Day.
Be surprising and creative.

Mother's Day

If I make a gift for Mom today,

"Thank you, _____," is what she'll say.

She likes to hear me _____

so I could _____.

She likes to watch me _____

so I could _____.

She likes to smell _____

so I could _____.

She likes to taste _____

so I could _____.

I'll pick a special, creative way
to give my mom a wonderful day!

by _____

Make a list poem about fun things to do in spring.

Spring Fun

Some things are fun to do alone:

_____

_____

_____

Some things are fun to do in pairs:

_____

_____

_____

Some things are fun to do in groups:

_____

_____

_____

Springtime fun
for everyone!

by _____

Write a poem about an insect talent show.
Use details to describe what you imagine.

Questions to think about:

What do the insects do in their show?
Do they sing, act, or do magic tricks?
Do they dance or play instruments?
What do they wear?

This has no details:	This has details:
The bees sing.	*The bees wore red bowties and buzzed a song about honey.*

Spring Talent Show

The spiders _____

_____.

The flies _____

_____.

The ladybugs _____

_____.

The mosquitoes _____

_____.

And the bumblebee

dressed in a bright purple cap

and tappity-tapped a musical rap.

by _____

The farmers market in the summer is full of fresh fruit and vegetables.

Write a riddle about one of the fresh foods for sale.

Give three clues in your riddle.

Example: *I am more orange than a peach.*
But I have no fur.
My juice may end up
all over your shirt.

What am I? *a nectarine*

From the Farmers Market

_____

_____

_____

_____

_____

What am I? _____

by _____

What you would like to do with and for your dad on Father's Day?
Organize your ideas here. Put the best one last.

_____

_____

_____

_____

_____

Recipe for a Fabulous Father's Day

1. My Dad and I could _____

_____.

2. Mix in some time when we _____

_____.

3. Add _____

_____.

4. End with a hug and a big high five.

That is my Father's Day recipe.

Hooray for Dad. Yippee! Yippee!

by _____

Write a poem about animals at a pond.
Put a number before each animal.
Use verbs that sparkle to describe
how the animals move.
You can use verbs from the box,
or make up your own.

Example: *5 mosquitoes whizzle*

Verbs That Sparkle:			
bound	glide	scramble	swoop
flit	jigger	skitter	wiggle
flutter	leap	slither	zip

At the Pond

89 mosquitoes _____.

_____ snakes _____.

_____ tadpoles _____.

_____ rabbits _____.

_____ butterflies _____.

_____ mice _____.

_____ water spiders _____.

_____ children _____.

by _____

Write a poem to say goodbye to different things at school.
Use alliteration—words that begin with the same sound.
Repeat the same sound as much as you can.

Example: *Goodbye to <u>r</u>unning at <u>r</u>ecess.*
Goodbye to <u>l</u>aughing at <u>l</u>unch.

Here is a list of things you might say goodbye to:

books	friends	library	teachers
classroom pets	late slips	recess	tests

Goodbye!

Goodbye to _____.

Goodbye to _____.

Goodbye to _____.

Hello to _____

_____!

by _____

Write a poem about the Fourth of July.

Try to use rhyming words that are in the middle of a line, instead of at the end.

Example: *On the Fourth of **July**,*
*the sky creates **eye** pictures.*

Here are some rhyming words to help you get started:

by	July	excite	quite
eye	my	ignite	right
firefly	spy	meteorite	sight
fly	sky	moonlight	twilight
high	why	night	white

The Fourth of July

by _____

Use your senses to describe a **summer picnic.**

Write about what you might see, smell, taste, hear, and touch.

You do not need to use complete sentences.

Example: *Crackle-crunch of chips against my teeth.*
Sweet smell of honeysuckle floating in the air.

Summer Picnic

_____

_____ .

_____

_____ .

_____

_____ .

_____

_____ .

by _____

Use sound words to bring this pool poem to life.

Example: *Thrish, thrash, we kick our legs.*

Pool Sounds

Whenever it is hot, I think it is cool

to go with friends to our neighborhood pool.

_____,

we laugh and jump in.

_____,

we kick our legs and swim.

_____,

we hear underwater sounds.

_____,

we shout to friends all around.

_____,

the lifeguard whistle blows.

_____,

licking popsicles, sweet and cold.

Our noisy, fun day has come to an end.

The next hot day, we will do it again.

by _____

Remember a fun time you had in the summer.
Describe two or three things you remember about it.

Example: *We waded into the ice-cold lake,*
splashing and laughing,
until our arms and legs finally warmed up.

Possible summer memories:

fun with friends	*a day at the pool*
fun with family	*a day at the park*
a family vacation	*a day at the lake*
a trip to another country	*a day at the beach*

Remembering Summer

_____

_____.

_____

_____.

_____

_____.

_____

_____.

by _____

You can make a storm come to life.

Use verbs that make the parts of the storm seem alive.

Example: *Clouds puff themselves up and turn dark and angry.*

Rain taps on the window as if it wants to come inside.

Here are some verbs you might use:

bellow	crack	howl	puff	roar	shuffle	whip
burst	cry	knock	rap	shiver	tap	zap

Stormy Summer Day

We run inside from the rainstorm.

Rain _____.

Lightning _____.

Thunder _____.

Wind _____.

Trees _____.

The sun punches through the clouds.

We dash outside to play in new puddles.

by _____

Write a poem to compare swimming underwater to a visit to a castle.

Example: *Swimming underwater in the ocean is like a visit to a castle.*
The seaweeds are like flags waving on the castle walls.

Use these questions to get you thinking:

Who are the princesses?   Who is the court jester or the clown?
Who are the princes?   Who are the villagers?
Who are the horsemen?   What are the castle flags?

Underwater Castle

Swimming underwater in the ocean is like a visit to a castle.

I am the king and the _____ is like the queen.

_____.

_____.

_____.

_____.

The ocean is like a castle, gigantic and grand,

until I pop my head up and swim back to the land.

by _____

Imagine running back and forth through a water sprinkler.
Write a poem that shows words that go back and forth, too.

The Sprinkler

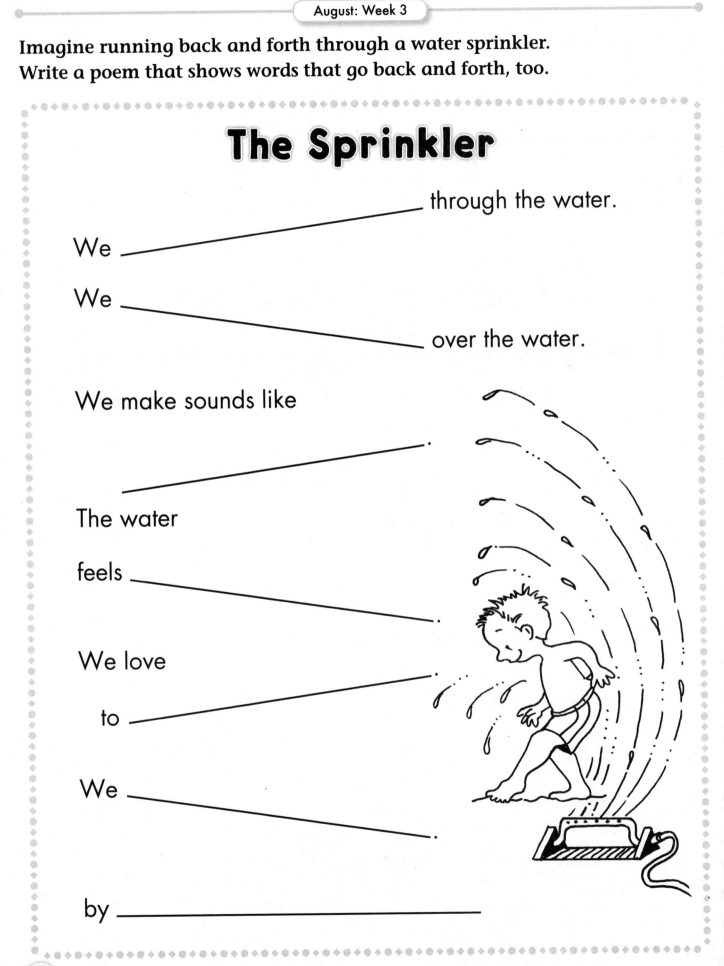

We ⟍⟋ through the water.

We ⟍ over the water.

We make sounds like ⟍

The water

feels ⟍

We love ⟍

to ⟍

We ⟍

by _____

Did you visit a library this summer?

Write about the different kinds of books you might have come across.

Fill in each verse with two book topics that are very different from each other.

Example: *Books on gorillas,*
books on stars.

Summer Reading

Books on _____,

books on _____.

Books on shelves are everywhere.

Books with _____,

and books with _____.

Big books here and small books there.

Books with people who _____

or _____

or _____.

The library books are here to share!

by _____

Write about yourself. Draw a picture to go with your poem.

My "Me" Poem

_____ is the color of my hair.

_____ is the color of my eyes.

Did you know I like to _____?

Or is that a big surprise?

I like to _____

with my family.

At _____

you might see my friends and me.

A book about _____

is what I like to read.

And I make a good friend.

Yes, indeed!

by _____

Write a "sound effects" poem!
Write the sounds you would hear.
Make up words if you want!

**Pick one of these ideas for
your poem:**

recess   school bus ride
airport   jungle
nighttime   drum practice

Here's an example:

Train Ride
"All abooooard!"
klang, kling
charooga, charooga
chooooo, chooooo
klickety-klack
down the track.

_____
(title)

_____

_____

_____

_____

_____

by _____

You are the reporter for the newspaper.
You are reporting on recess.
What do kids do at recess time?

Kids Have Fun at Recess

Hello, I am _____,
(your name)

and I'm bringing you the latest,

because recess at _____ School

is definitely the greatest!

Some kids are playing _____.

Others are _____.

And look at what this group is doing!

They are _____.

So that is all I have to report today.

I am _____,
(your name)

signing off to go and play!

Write a round poem! Pretend you are one of these round things:

yo-yo	*balloon*	*cake*	*soccer ball*
clock	*pizza*	*gumball*	*bubble*

Use these questions to help you write your poem:

What would you look like?　　*What would you spend time doing?*

How would you move?　　*What would people do with you?*

What would you be good at?　　*How would you feel?*

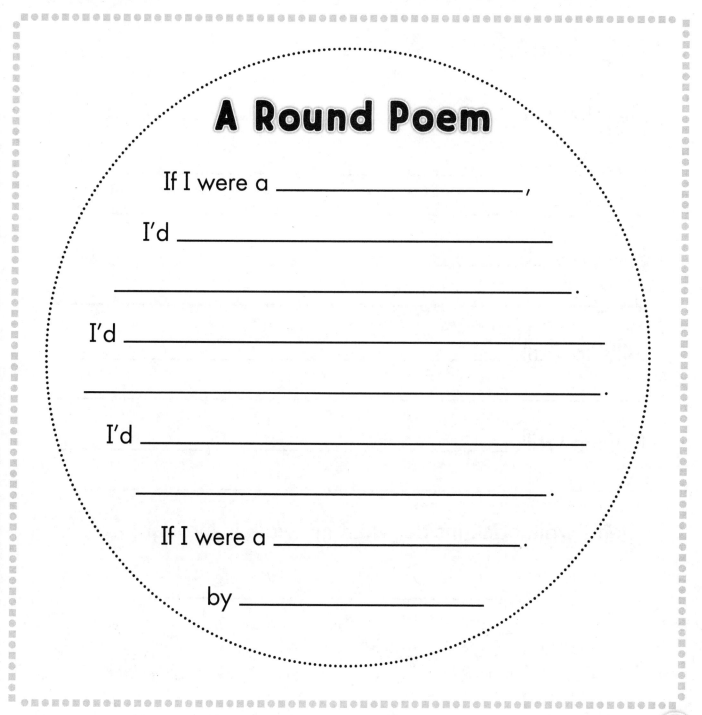

A Round Poem

If I were a _____,

I'd _____

_____.

I'd _____

_____.

I'd _____

_____.

If I were a _____.

by _____

What season is it? Picture an outdoor scene for that season.

Imagine taking a walk through your scene this week. Fill in the season in your poem. Then use intriguing words to describe your walk.

Example: *I like to walk barefoot through slippery grass.*

My Weekly Walk in _____
(season)

I like to walk outside in _____, it's true.

I like to walk _____

_____.

I like to walk _____

_____.

I like to walk _____

_____.

I like to walk _____

_____.

Then I walk back inside when my walk is through.

by _____

Write an action poem!
First, pick any animal or insect.
Then write only action words on
the lines to tell what it is doing.
Draw pictures near each word.

Example:

A Ladybug in Action!
crawling
creeping
exploring
flitting
flying
and good-bying!

A _____ in Action!

_____ ing

_____ ing

_____ ing

_____ ing

_____ ing

and good-bying!

by _____

Notes